Generations in the Garden

Nancy O'Donnell Stoddard

This book is lovingly published by

Crazy Mountain Publishing.

Generations in the Garden

by Nancy O'Donnell Stoddard

Published July 2017

ISBN 9781548460686

Generations in the Garden

Foreword

Chapter One

Chapter Two

Chapter Three

Foreword

L to R Rear - Uncle Fred Autrey, Aunt Ellen Autrey, Stella Riddlemoser, Bonnie Autrey, Blanche Autrey, Fred Autrey, Duane Autrey

L to R Front - Nancy O'Donnell, Clara O'Donnell holding Terry O'Donnell, Kathy O'Donnell

My family were all gardeners. Everyone I can remember raised some plants. My grandparents raised huge gardens out of necessity. That was how people ate in my world. My very early years were colored by WWII. Everyone had a Victory Garden to eke out their rationing stamps. There were no home freezers in those days, so everyone canned their produce. Many farmers raised vegetables and would bring their produce to town to sell. Many times my grandmother would buy bushel baskets of tomatoes, peas or green beans and she, my mother and my Aunt Ellen would can them. Everyone brought their own canning jars and worked together to fill them. My spot would be to sit under the kitchen table (three women rushing around in my grandmother's small kitchen were dangerous for small children) and my job would be to snap beans or shell peas.

Grandpa Autrey raised chickens, turkeys and rabbits. I don't remember ever going without meat, but many people did. Grandpa raised meat for three families. My Dad fished and hunted for ducks and pheasants. Uncle Fred would hunt with him, so our families never had "meatless Tuesdays" as many people did during WWII. Mom canned fish and pheasants. However, I don't remember eating a hamburger until I was in Junior High School.

My Grandfather O'Donnell was a coal miner. He was injured in the mine and was forced to retire. This happened after my Grandmother died. Ed had remarried and had a second family to support. His wife got a job and he did odd jobs and raised an enormous garden to help provide for his family. He raised the best strawberries I ever tasted. They were Ogallala and Ozark Beauty. Those are the varieties that I raise to this day.

G.E. and Clara Autrey O'Donnell C. 1936

My Father and Mother raised roses and African violets. Both my parents were national rose judges.

They also provided test gardens for several rose companies. Most of the Brownell Sub-Zero Roses were tested in their rose beds. They hybridized African Violets and named them for relatives. There was a Nancy, Kathy, Bonnie and Ellen. Their yard was a show place with gorgeous flower beds. Daddy also raised peonies and was active in establishing the Denver Botanical Garden. He contributed the original reference material on the cultivation of peonies to the garden's library. The summer following his death, my Mother and I visited the Garden. I asked for information about peonies because we were raising peonies at that time. They gave me copies of Daddy's handwritten notes copied on a copier.

Chapter One

Soil

Your garden soil is the most important factor in the success of gardening. The tools for soil analysis and amendment are some of the first things to purchase. You will need to determine the ph of your soil first. For this process you will need a soil sample to test. You can obtain this sample by digging with a trowel or a plug tool. You need to dig at varying depths and place the dirt in a plastic bag. I recommend digging in the top 6" of your garden soil and getting at least 12 small samples. Mix them in the bag in order to have an average ph result. In Montana, you can go to the office of your County Extension Agent with a request that your sample be sent to the State Office for analysis. It is also a good idea to send a water sample from the source that you will be using to irrigate your garden.

The ideal result would be 6.5 to 7 which is a neutral reading. Higher ph indicates alkaline soil or water and lower indicates acidic soil or water. You can treat soil with gypsum to lower the ph and lime to raise it. Water can't be treated but you can treat the soil so that you don't have residual effects from using alkaline or acidic water.

When the ph is too high or too low, some nutrients are locked in the soil and not available to your plants. When the leaves of your plants turn yellow, your plants are lacking iron or possibly nitrogen. Examine a leaf. If you see green veins with yellow between the veins, they need iron. If the whole leaf is yellow, the plants are not getting enough nitrogen. Nitrogen deficiency is easily treated with a fertilizer. Iron deficiency is more difficult to correct. Some specific iron supplements for plants are very strong and will either burn or kill the plant if not carefully applied. Usually, iron sources that are added when you are preparing the garden in the spring or putting it to bed in the fall are safest for your plants. You may have to test your soil and adjust the ph to release the iron in the soil. We have found that a lawn fertilizer spreader is a great way to spread gypsum. Since the soil here is alkaline we have to use gypsum periodically.

Following is a chart that illustrates alkalinity and acidity of your garden soil. It shows the trace minerals and shows what ph makes them available to your plants.

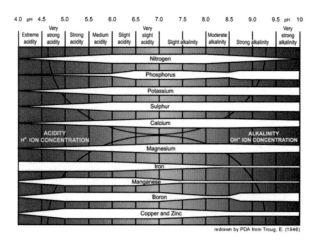

redrawn by PDA from Troug, E. (1946)

You want to add humus to your soil. You can create truly great gardening soil by mulching the garden and tilling the mulch under when you clean up and till your soil in the fall. Any ground-up organic material such as hay, straw, grass clippings or leaves makes good mulch or humus. I grind hay and use it to mulch the garden, building up 6 inches of mulch for most of my garden.

Compost

I think adding leaves to the mulch is important because trees pull up nutrients from deep in the soil and are an excellent source of trace elements. Compost is a very positive addition to the soil.

Making compost is time consuming but so beneficial to your soil, it is very worthwhile. There is cold composting which involves putting everything compostable in a pile or bin. Be sure it has plenty of air. Stir it periodically, especially if

4

you add a large amount of something like leaves or grass clippings. You can add all your vegetable waste but avoid any meat, fat or oil.

There is hot composting which involves more work, but produces finished compost in a lot less time.

The following method should give you a 3-foot pile of compost in 21 to 28 days and every 7 days thereafter. To make compost efficiently you need a shredder grinder. You also need a long soil thermometer and three bins. The bins can be made inexpensively by using pallets. Set four fence posts in a square. Distance the posts so that you can wire the pallets to the posts making a square container. Fasten the front pallet so that you can open it like a gate. Set two posts so that you can wire three more pallets to them creating a gate with the front pallet. Create a third bin in the same way, so that you have three bins side by side. Each should open to the front.

Open the first bin. Run your compostable material through the shredder grinder. Layer it in the first bin. Make a 6" layer of green material (grass clippings are perfect). Then a 6" layer of brown material (ground leaves, hay and straw work well). Then layer dirt and/or manure. We prefer manure. Spray with water until the material is the consistency of a wrung out sponge. You can purchase an inoculant to speed up decomposition from a garden center or garden catalog. Repeat the layers until you have a 3' pile. If you live in a rainy area, you may want to use a breathable tarp to cover the pile. Take the temperature of your pile daily. It should heat up to 160 or $170^{o.}$

When the temperature begins to lower, it is time to transfer the material to the second bin. This mixes the material and adds oxygen to the mix. If it needs water to keep it the consistency of a wrung-out sponge, spray it with water. Create a new pile in the first bin using the same method as the first one. Use a shovel full of the compost from the first batch to inoculate the second batch. Again, take the temperature of both bins daily. When the temperature drops, repeat the process. You should have finished compost in the third bin in 21 to 28 days after starting the process. This was Bert's method and he produced great compost.

Chapter Two

Planting

Planning your garden is a wonderful way to spend a cold, snowy winter day. Never plant a vegetable in the same location two years in a row. Rotate your crops religiously. Amending your soil with compost, mulch and fertilizer keeps a greedy plant from using up nutrients in the garden. Green beans and peas fix nitrogen in the soil. Corn is very greedy so I put a tablespoon of fertilizer beneath the seeds. I dig my planting holes deep enough so that I can put dirt between the seeds and the fertilizer. I do the same for my tomato seedlings.

In the fall, Bert uses a tractor and plows the garden area or chisels the soil. Then he discs it to break up the clods. A roto-tiller will do the same job. You want to break up the soil and work the mulch and compost into the dirt. Sending the garden into the winter tilled up allows the mulch and compost to break up in the soil and absorb any amendments (gypsum, iron or fertilizer). It also allows it to absorb water from the snow.

I draw a master plan each winter and then after tilling the soil each spring, I mark my rows with big nails or lengths of rebar. I use a yardstick to place the row markers. I stretch sisal string between the markers and along the rows so I have the proper spacing for my planting. I carry a 6" ruler and/or a yardstick when I am planting so I can plant the seeds or seedlings with healthy spacing. I also place a rake and a hoe at the end of the rows. I smooth the soil with the rake and the hoe is dragged along the sisal line to mark the rows with a tiny ditch. I leave the markers and sisal in place to mark the rows until the seeds sprout. I also mark the rows and part rows with vegetable markers to indicate what is planted there.

Photo by Brad Stoddard

Bert sets fence posts and attaches hog wire or chicken wire to the posts so that my peas can climb up the fencing. I have found that if you have the right kind of weather in the fall, you can get two crops of peas. I got lazy one year and didn't clean up the pea vines. They lived all summer and I was shocked to see them blooming in September. I got a second crop of peas a few weeks later.

For the squash and cucumbers and melons, I dig a hole to place a bottomless bucket. I cut the bottom out of 5 gallon buckets. I dig them in 6 feet apart in rows 6 feet apart. I fill each of them with potting soil mixed with compost until the filling measures 3" to 4" from the top. I mark each bucket with a separate marker to indicate the variety of cucumber or squash I plant in them. The aim is to plant five seeds in a circle in each bucket. I plant 6 buckets of cucumbers and 25 or 26 of winter squash. One bucket is used for Zucchini. This part of the garden is watered by hand by filling the buckets with water from a hose. The water is concentrated on the roots of each plant and I don't waste water by sprinkling the huge area between

11

buckets. During the hot part of the summer, I fill the buckets 3 times a week.

My irrigation system for the rest of the garden consists of 6 raised platforms with an oscillating sprinkler wired to each. The sprinklers are set up with two spaced about 6' from the EW edges of the garden. Each pair is about 1/3 of the way from the North edge of the garden. I have a manifold system that feeds water to one pair of sprinklers at a time. Depending on the weather, I time it to change pairs of sprinklers every 3 hours. I try to have overlapping sprinklers on the corn because it is the tallest vegetable. The squash buckets are placed at

the North or South edge of the garden each year because they are planted in fresh soil each year and don't utilize nutrients from the same soil every year. I put time release pellets of fertilizer in each. After planting, sprinkle and keep the ground moist to enable seeds to sprout. Don't water to the point of washing out the seed. Just keep the ground moist.

Insect Pests

I try to attract bees and other pollinators to my garden. I plant borage to attract bees. My Grandmother used to say, "Borage calls out to the bees," and she was right. When the plants bloom, the whole row will vibrate from the bees working the blossoms. Bert mows the rows that are through producing. One year he was mowing the borage and was stung by bees that didn't approve. Bees are so important to producing vegetables and fruit, it would be counter-productive to spray insecticides and kill them. So, I try to fool the pests.

I protect the susceptible plants by using panty hose to keep out the cabbage moths. I crawl the rows of potatoes (wearing cushy knee pads) with a pair of needle nosed pliers. I crunch the potato beetles with my pliers. I also turn over every potato leaf to check for beetle eggs. They are bright orange as are the beetles. I tear off any leaf with eggs and drop it into a coffee can with gasoline in it. It makes a nice little fire when I am finished.

When my chokecherry trees have tent caterpillars I break off the affected branches and burn them. I have a row of wild roses along the South fence of the garden. One year they were showing signs of Rose Gauls. I think it is spread by grasshoppers and other insects. I tried just breaking off the stems that had gauls and burning them. It didn't work so I just cut off every bush to about 2" above the ground. I burned all the resultant debris. The next summer they all grew back and gaul has not been a problem since.

It is a lot of work, but well worth the effort. I don't want to eat fruit or vegetables that have residual insecticides on them. The one exception I make is to make a line of Golden Malrin around the base of every fruit tree to combat ants who bring aphids to my fruit trees. I have never seen a bee on the Malrin, so I think we are safe there. I also spray

Sevin on the cucumbers and squash when powdery mildew attacks the leaves. I used sawdust as mulch one year and introduced powdery mildew to my garden.

My grandparents raised chicken and turkeys. Each year they turned the chickens into the garden before planting. They had a lot fewer insect pests when they did this. The chickens see the insect eggs and clean them out for you. They also are hungry for fresh greens and do a good job of weeding.

Seed Tapes

Seed tapes are a great way to save money on seeds. I make seed tapes for carrots, turnips, green onions, cocktail onions and beets. I make them from the cheapest flimsiest toilet paper I can find. This year I made them from Scott's cheapest paper. I use a ballpoint pen, Elmer's glue, a quilter's tiny glue point (sold for applique glue), some saved centers from paper towel rolls, my 4' quilting ruler and toothpicks. I roll out the paper on my 7' table. I mark the underside end of the paper with the name of the seeds I am using. I use my quilting ruler to mark the spacing for the seeds. I mark them down the center of the paper. At first, I tried to cut down the center of the paper to make the tapes narrower. It wasn't worth the extra time it took. I mark a line of dots where the seeds should be placed. For example, the spacing of carrot seeds is every 4". I break off the paper at the end of the table. My garden rows are 42' long, so I need 6 tapes. I put the fine quilting point on the glue. I then put a very tiny spot of glue on the marks for the first 2' of the paper. I pour out some carrot seeds onto a sheet of white paper. I dip a toothpick in a very small bowl of water and use the wet pointed end to pick up a carrot seed. I then place the carrot seed on the first spot of glue. I continue the process until I finish the 7' strip. I push the strip aside to dry. I try to use as little glue and water as I can. After I complete 6 tapes, I allow 30 minutes for them to dry and then I fold them and wind them around a paper towel center which has been marked with the seed name. This is the perfect way to get even spacing on tiny seeds.

When I am ready to plant them, I just place them in the little ditch that I make with the hoe. I then cover them with dirt and firm it with my foot. I have never had a failure with these seed tapes.

Following is a chart showing Soil Temperatures for planting: Cool-Season Crops

Vegetable	Germination Temperature °F minimum/optimum/maximum
Beets	40°/80°/90°
+Broccoli	40°/80°/90°
+Cabbage	40°/80°/90°
Carrots	40°/80°/90°
Cauliflower	40°/80°/90°
Leeks	40°/80°/90°
Lettuce	35°/70°/70°
Onions, green	35°/80°/90°
Onions, dry sets	35°/80°/90°
Parsnips	35°/70°/90°
Peas	40°/70°/80°
Potatoes	45° and up
Radishes	40°/80°/90°
Spinach	40°/70°/70°
Swiss chard	40°/85°/95°
Turnips	40°/80°/100°

Warm-Season Crops

Vegetable	Germination Temperature °F minimum/optimum/maximum
Beans	55°/80°/90°
Cantaloupe	60°/90°/100°
Corn	50°/80°/100°
Cucumbers	60°/90°/100°
+Eggplant	60°/80°/90°

+Peppers	60°/80°/90°
+Tomato	50°/80°/100°
Squash	60°/90°/100°
Watermelons	60°/90°/110°

* Source: Colorado State University Horticulture Extension
+ Usually planted as established seedlings, not as seed.

Buy a good soil thermometer. It will make a big difference in the success of your planting and germination.

Chapter Three

Fruit Trees

I have wild plums, chokecherries, Nanking Cherries, pie cherries (Romeo and Carmine Jewel), Sweet Sixteen apples, Contender peaches, Chestnut crabapples and several crabapples I don't know the name of. Wild plums and chokecherries sucker and you can dig and plant suckers if you need to replace any of the trees. The main issue with planting fruit trees is watering them. I have two watering systems for the trees. The plums and chokecherries are planted in ditches so I put a hose in the ditches and let the water run all day to water those trees.

Wild plums ready to make
into jelly

The domestic fruit trees each are watered with a bucket system. I take a five-gallon bucket with a lid. In the lower three inches of the side of the bucket drill a 1" round hole. Attach a beer spigot with a handle. I order mine from Amazon or pick them up from a business that sells beer making supplies.

Dig a $10 hole for a $5 tree. Bert uses a posthole digger powered by a tractor to dig holes for the trees. I fill the hole with water and let it seep away. Then I mix compost and manure to fill the hole. Again, I water it. During this time, I also put the bare root trees in a bucket of water for 24 hours before I plant them. The next day I plant the trees leaving a basin in the dirt around the base of the tree. I place the bucket so that the spigot sticks out over the basin. I fill the bucket with water and set the spigot to drip the water into the basin. If, in four or five weeks, the trees don't bud and leaf out, I "shock" the tree by cutting a few inches off the main stem. That will usually cause the tree to leaf out.

I put a brick inside each bucket to keep them from blowing over when they are empty of water. At the end of the growing season, I scrub them with Clorox to kill any algae they have picked up. I also remove the spigot and store them in my garden shed. The buckets can be stacked for use the following summer. Most fruit trees that are listed as self-pollinating will bear much more heavily if there is another tree of the same variety nearby. However, the Chestnut Crabapple tree is a universal pollinator for apple trees and crabapples alike.

Asparagus

Asparagus is a perennial. An asparagus bed, once established, can last for 20+ years. Plant the roots in the spring. Allow to grow that year and the next. In the second year just pick one spear from each plant. During the third year and every year thereafter, pick 50% of the spears. Top dress with mulch and compost. Then leave alone.

Do not use salt on the bed. Salting asparagus is an "old wife's tale". Asparagus is tolerant of salt, not in need of salt.

Beans

Green Beans will germinate 100% if the soil temperature is 80° However, if you live in an area that has a shorter growing season you might have to plant when the soil temperature is lower. Placing black plastic on the ground where you plan to plant will speed up soil warming. Plant the seeds 1 ½ inches deep with 4" between plants. Rows should be 18-24 inches apart. If you soak your seeds overnight before planting it speeds up germination. I plant bush beans because creating a place for beans to climb doesn't work well in my garden. That is a personal preference. Pole beans are just as delicious. I pick every 4 or 5 days during the bearing season. Canning or freezing the same day as picking is preferable. The flavor is much better. When I cook fresh green beans, I boil to tender crisp with diced bacon. I also cook the beans while I sauté bacon pieces and chopped onion. Then I drain the beans and mix with the bacon and onions.

Beets

Beets work well for homemade seed tapes. Plant them 2-3 inches apart with 12" between the rows. Every beet seed combines 4-5 actual seeds so you may want to thin them. They have a thick skin. Pull

beets. Wash off all the soil and trim the leaves 2"
from the beet. Boil for 30 minutes. Pour into a
colander and allow to cool. You can slip the peel off
along with the root and stems. I slice them and
heat with butter, sugar and a little vinegar. They
are really good. If you want to make pickled beets,
peel, slice and can in vinegar solution. I also slice
some onions and alternate them in the jar with the
sliced beets. When you open the jar, the beets will
have colored the onion and It makes a very
attractive relish plate.

Borage

Borage is easy to grow and volunteers the next year
all over the garden. It seeds itself in unexpected
places. You can either plant it again or let it grow
where it will. It will not conform to symmetry or
control. It dies if you try to transplant it. It will add
whimsy to your regimented garden. Plant it 3"
apart in a row down the center of the garden. From
the next year on, you will find it growing
everywhere.

Broccoli

Plant the seedlings 36" apart with rows 36" from each other. One broccoli plant will produce heads after the main head has been cut. Allow the little heads to develop after cutting the big head. Keep a close eye on them and don't allow them to develop into yellow flowers. You can cut indefinitely on each plant if you watch them carefully. Soak the harvested broccoli in salt water to eliminate cabbage worms. Rinse.

Broccoli freezes well. I use slightly cooked broccoli in salads. It tastes better if you cook it just a tad. Use butter on it or use cheese sauce for a vegetable dish. As you can tell, I am not what you could call a low calorie cook

Brussel Sprouts

Brussel sprouts are so mild when cooked fresh. I like to grow Long Island seedlings. Plant the seedlings 2 feet apart in rows 3' apart. Each plant creates a long stalk. At the point when the stalk makes a leaf it will form a sprout. To get maximum growth of the sprouts, break off the leaf. Leave only the leaves at the top end of the stalk. All the growth will go to the sprouts. They are delicious when cooked until tender and butter melted on them. Not exactly fat free but really taste good. They are also good with your choice of salad dressing. They freeze well. I freeze them on a cookie sheet and after frozen put them in a plastic freezer bag.

Cabbage

Cabbage is very easy to grow. I like Early Jersey Wakefield. Plant the seedlings 24" apart. Since I have plenty of space, I make my rows 24" apart. To avoid the holes and green worms, I enclose the head in knee length pantyhose as soon as it forms. There is plenty of stretch in the hose so that the head can grow to full size while enclosed. You want to get it enclosed before the white moths appear. To get rid of any cabbage worms you soak your harvested cabbage heads in salt water. The green worms will often float to the top of the water. Peel off the outside leaves and you will get any eggs that remain.

I make sauerkraut from the cabbages. You can control the sour flavor if you make your own. I make it in a stainless-steel kettle and use a sawed-off baseball bat to pound the cabbage. I mix it with salt and then pound it. When it is full of juice, pour it into the crock. Cover the crock with a plate. Then drape a dishtowel over the crock. Stir the contents daily. Taste it periodically and when it reaches the flavor your family likes, can it. It makes great Reuben Sandwiches. I also have a recipe for sauerkraut salad that is delicious. Open 1 pint sauerkraut. Mix with 2 chopped green onions and ½ C chopped celery. Dress with 1 C oil, ½ C sugar & ¼ C vinegar.

Carrots

Carrots require a ground temperature of 50° but can be planted at a lower temperature. The germination rate will be lower. I plant my carrots using home-made seed tapes. I plant Scarlet Nantes because they freeze well. I freeze them shredded in 2 cup amounts and sliced in ½ cup portions. This is perfect for carrot cake or 1 cup makes a great addition to coleslaw or stir-fry, ½ C is perfect for stew.

Cauliflower

Cauliflower from the garden is delicious. However, it is very difficult to harvest WHITE cauliflower. I try to catch the seedling when the head first begins to form. Catch some leaves wrapped around the head and enclose them in knee length pantyhose. Don't believe the claim that the variety is self-blanching. They lie. Achieving heads of white cauliflower has been my greatest gardening challenge.

Plant the seedlings 24" apart and in rows 30" apart. I plant my broccoli, brussels sprouts, cabbage and cauliflower in the same area or rows. Try to enclose the head before the white moths appear. Soak the heads in salt water to float out the cabbage worms and eggs. I freeze cauliflower the day I harvest. I serve it cooked and smothered with cheese sauce.

Celery

I plant celery seedlings. I do not blanch it. We like it fresh from the garden and green. I think it has more flavor than the blanched celery you buy from the grocery store. I only plant a few seedlings because I have had poor luck with freezing celery. My grandparents had a dirt basement that they used as a root cellar. They had a Hoosier cabinet in the cellar. Grandma used it to store canning jars. There were always 2 crocks of pickles sitting on the cabinet. One of sweet and one of dill. Every fall Grandpa would fill the pull-out flour bin in the cabinet with damp sand. He would bury carrots and celery in the damp sand. I can remember digging out carrots or celery for Grandma to cook. Remember, this was before freezers.

Plant the seedlings 12" apart. You may have to tie the stems loosely to keep them from sprawling. Celery doesn't like heat and may go to seed if your summer is very hot.

Corn

Corn should be planted when the soil temperature is 60° If the temperature is lower, expect spotty germination. However, if you need to plant earlier, as long as you plant in a five row grid, spotty germination is not a problem for pollination. You will still get a corn crop, just not as numerous. A five row grid is the most effective way to get your corn to pollinate.

Choosing your corn seed is a major decision. Corn varieties are designated as su (sugary) se (sugar enhanced) and sh2 (shrunken super sweet). I prefer se because they retain the sugar in the kernels for a week or sometimes 2 after picking. Su varieties sometimes begin to convert the sugar into starch in as little as 2 hours. If you plant an se variety, you must be sure there is no other variety planted within 300 feet. Corn is a wind pollinator and wind drift is a cause of cross pollination. You may end up with inedible corn if it cross pollinates with another less sugary variety.

I always plant 3 seeds in each planting hole. Plant corn 12" apart in rows 30-36" apart. Dig a planting hole at least 1 ½ to 2" deep. I dig my holes deeper and put a tablespoon of fertilizer in the hole. I put some dirt on top of the fertilizer and firm it with the handle end of my trowel. Then I drop in the seeds. Plant in a block of at least 4 rows. I prefer 5 rows and never have a problem with pollination. You can plant two varieties if you wait to plant the second until the earlier variety has at least 3 leaves before planting the second. Water immediately and keep the soil damp until the seeds sprout. Mulch deeply after sprouting. Mulch after weeding. This will help keep weeds down.

We also let some corn dry on the stalk each year. We use it to feed the cottontail rabbits, sharptail grouse, and pheasants at the shop and the house.

Cucumbers

When I plant in the buckets, I usually plant 8 seeds and if they all sprout I try to pick out the 5 strongest plants and thin the other three. However, I am so thrilled by sprouted seeds that sometimes I wimp out and leave all 8 growing. Do as I say, not as I do. I also use some time release fertilizer pellets in each bucket.

I plant Straight Eight and National Pickling seeds. I really don't see the point in growing "burpless" cucumbers. They don't taste different and we love to eat any fresh picked cucumbers. When I find the first two little finger sized cucumbers, we treat ourselves by eating them. I make lots of them into pickles and we eat them fresh. I make a crock of 14 day sweet pickles and then grind them to can into sweet relish. Add some onion when you grind them. It makes great relish.

Lettuce

I plant a lettuce mix. They grow for such a short time here that I don't make a seed tape of them. Our weather turns too hot for lettuce. Some years I plant some again the first of September. If I get lucky they are up and large enough to harvest before the first killing frost. I harvest with a pair of shears because they grow again if I don't pull up the plants. I cut enough for a large bag of lettuce. I soak them in a large pan and rinse the leaves individually. I put the rinsed lettuce on a towel to soak up some of the water. Then I put the rinsed leaves in a large piece of nylon netting. Think prom dress skirt back in the day. I carry it out to the sidewalk and twirl it to get rid of more water. My kids were so afraid their friends would see me twirling a net full of lettuce around my head. Then put it in a large plastic bag and refrigerate. You have great salad for a week.

Melon

The only melon I have been able to raise is Sugar Baby. It is a short season melon and ripens here. I raise it in a bottomless bucket. One year I raised Mouse Melons. They are about the size of a small egg but we couldn't tell when they were ripe so I just stick to Sugar Baby. I have raised Minnesota Midget Cantaloupe very successfully, but no one in my family cares for cantaloupe so I gave them up.

Okra

I raise Okra just for myself. I raise Clemson Spineless. I think I would raise Okra just to have the seeds. They are a beautiful blue. The flowers are beautiful also. However, I love Okra so I would raise it if it had ugly seeds. Plant 2-4" apart in rows 3' apart. The soil temperature should be 70°. I pull off the pods when they are only 2-3" long. Nobody wants Okra that is tough and spiny and it gets that way fast. I pick every day because it matures very quickly. I cook it with crushed tomatoes, chopped green peppers and sautéed onions. Sometimes with chicken broth and rice. It is great in jambalaya.

Onions

I raise yellow onions, green bunching onions and pearl onions for pickling. I make seed tapes for the bunching onions and pearl onions.

Plant the onion sets 5" apart. Make the rows 12" apart. When the tops of the yellow onions fall over (sometimes they need a little help) and turn brown I pull them and let them harden on a tarp beside the garden. When they have hardened for about a week and they have yellow-brown skin on the outside, I sort out the ones I think will be keepers and store them in a cardboard box in my basement. I use a lot of onions and I usually grow and harvest enough to keep for 5 or 6 months. I just buy the yellow onion sets that are sold in the grocery stores.

For green bunching onions, I raise the Lisbon Bunching Onions. I make seed tapes for these. Plant them 2" apart. We use a lot of them and I usually have enough in the garden to last all summer.

For cocktail onions, I raise Cipollini white onions. Plant them 2" apart. They grow well from seed tapes. They need to have the tops semi broken and laid to the side to pearl. I just use my feet to break and lay over the tops. When the tops turn brown they are usually shaped like pearls. These don't usually form a paper skin. You just have to cut off the roots and top and wash them well to pickle them. I use them for relish plates for holiday dinners. Another onion that pearls well is Eclipse.

Peas

I prefer Wando. Peas are planted early so that they can mature in cooler weather. Bert builds me a fence out of metal fence posts with hog wire fastened to the posts. I plant the peas 2" apart. I also plant on both sides of the fence. One year I did not clean up the plants and just let them live all summer. Conditions were perfect that fall – cool days but no killing frost and I got a second crop of peas. Since then I let them grow all summer and have gotten a second crop twice. If I pick a bunch of pods, wash them and put them in a bowl on the kitchen counter my children and grandchildren will empty the bowl in a few hours. I freeze the peas in

1 Cup amounts. They are perfect for an addition to a salad, soup or a stew.

Peppers

Jalapenos are easy to grow. Plant seedlings 12" apart. They are tropical plants and when the nights are below 50° they tend to sulk and are slow to bloom, so put them in last of all the seedlings. You can plant them and tomatoes at the same time. Slice them and pickle them and/or use them to make jalapeno jelly. I pour the jelly over softened cream cheese and serve it with crackers for appetizers.

Potatoes

You can purchase seed potatoes at a grocery store or garden center. We prefer Yukon Gold and Kennebec. Traditionally potatoes are planted on Good Friday. I do not cut up potatoes to plant. I think cutting potatoes results in a certain percentage of failure so I buy small seed potatoes and plant them whole. Plant the potatoes 12" apart and with rows 12" apart. First till the ground and amend it with fertilizer. Potatoes are greedy and need to be fed.

We don't plant potatoes in a traditional way. We place them on top of the ground and then pile mulch on top of them. We have piled 8" of mulch on top with both rows covered as one mulched bed. Then we unroll chicken wire on top of the mulch. We use tent stakes to fasten down the ends of the chicken wire. The result is a bed of mulch about 24" wide held down by chicken wire. Water well because the mulch will need to be damp to settle and keep moisture for the potatoes. The potato plants will push through the mulch and wire and leaf out. When they bloom, you can uncover one end and harvest some new potatoes. They are delicious cooked in some chicken broth.

Drain and then add half and half and some frozen peas. When potatoes are new you can scrub off the skins.

When you decide to harvest the crop, lay them beside the garden and spray them with a hose to remove dirt. Then lay them on a tarp to harden. Cover them at night if frost is predicted. Leave them out for several days to harden completely. You may have to turn them to be sure they are hardened on both sides

Traditional planting methods bury the seed potatoes 3" deep in rows 36" apart. These potatoes will have to be dug. We prefer to grow them unburied. You will have to dig some of them but most of them will be on top of the ground or easily dug up.

Pumpkins

Pumpkins are grown in bottomless buckets. I grow small sweet pie pumpkins. I buy Connecticut Pie Pumpkin seeds. I also raise Jack B Little decorative pumpkins. I paint faces and put raffia wigs on the pie pumpkins for Halloween and then cook them and freeze the meat for holiday pies. Use tempera paint so you can wash it off. I plant 8 and thin to 5.

Rhubarbs

Rhubarb is a perennial. The ideal location for rhubarb is along the sides of a shed or building of some kind so that the rain falling off the roof waters the plants. Plant roots in the spring. Prepare the soil with lots of humus and compost. I prefer solid red rhubarb so I like Valentine or Canada Red. Let the roots establish for several years before picking. Only pick 1/3 of the stalks. Also, pick the stalks before they bloom. You can extend the season by cutting off the blooms before they open. Rhubarb freezes well and you don't have to scald or blanch the rhubarb before freezing. Just wash it and cut it up and freeze it.

Spinach

I grow Bloomsdale which, although fast to bolt, is delicious. I don't make a seed tape for it because it lasts about as long as the lettuce. I harvest it with shears and treat it as I do the lettuce.

Squash

The only summer squash I raise is one bucket of Zucchini. We like it sautéed, raw and in mock apple bars or zucchini bread. We really like winter squash. I raise Sweet Mama, Spaghetti Squash, Blue Hubbard, Waltham Butternut and Buttercup. Our favorite is Sweet Mama. Robbin taught me a great way to cut open Spaghetti squash. Pierce it with a fork in a line that you wish to cut. Cut along the line. Clean the seeds out and bake on a cookie sheet with the cut sides down. I have a hatchet to cut the Blue Hubbard. I use the Waltham Butternut baked and in soup with onions and garlic.

Squash blossoms can be hand pollinated. At the base of the female flowers is a swelling. The male blossoms do not have this swelling. You can use a make-up brush or a child's paint brush to remove pollen from a male flower and pollenate a female flower. Try it and see the result. The articles on this subject call for a camel's hair artists brush. I have used a child's brush that came with a tin of tempera. It works just fine. I have also taken a blossom from a fruit tree and just smooshed it into another blossom and it worked. I don't know how to tell gender on fruit tree blossoms. If the bees aren't in your garden some year, it can make your crop.

When the first frost knocks down the leaves on the squash vines, cut the stems of the squash to no less than 2 inches from the vegetable. I use a hand pruner. If the stem breaks off flush with the vegetable, cook them shortly because they will rot in a few weeks. Pick all the squash and pumpkins and put them on a tarp beside the garden to ripen and harden. Even those that are still green will ripen if handled this way. Cover the squash with a blanket if frost is forecast. Treat pumpkins in the same way. Let them harden for at least 5 days.

Photo credit Bert Stoddard

Sweet Potatoes

Against all advice I plant sweet potatoes. I raise Georgia Jets. They are the fastest sweet potatoes to mature. The supplier of the plants needs a phone call to assure them that I know they need to send them to me before the planting time in my zone. Sometimes they need several phone calls. Sometimes I need to nag. I plant the slip under a gallon milk jug that has the bottom cut out. It makes a great mini-greenhouse. Take off the lid during the day and put it on at night. As soon as the temperature stays hot, take off the milk jugs. I don't dig them until the first killing frost. They are small but delicious.

I till the bed and add lots of compost. I use black plastic on the ground where they will be planted so the soil warms earlier. I plant the slips 12" apart and try to protect them from any cold spell. A blanket over the milk jugs is good protection if the weather turns cold.

Tomatoes

Tomatoes are also tropical and should not be set out before nighttime temperatures are at least 50°. However, I set mine out under gallon milk jugs with the bottom cut off. Put the lid on at night and take it off during the day. Build a circular support out of hog wire. It should be 24" in diameter and at least 30" tall. Remove the lowest circular wire. This leaves stakes at the bottom that you can sink in the ground to stabilize the support. These keep the tomatoes off the ground and gives them support when you have a storm.

In our soil, blossom end rot is a problem. I solve this by planting a tomato that is resistant to this problem. Celebrity is the variety I plant. I also plant four yellow pear tomato plants. I reward myself for weeding by picking and eating the yellow pear tomatoes. I also plant several grape tomatoes for salads but I have 36 Celebrity plants because I can a lot of ketchup and plain tomatoes. I peel the tomatoes and run them through the blender. I can this juice in the largest jars I can buy and sterilize. I process it in my cold pack canner. This juice can be used in stew and soup and spaghetti sauce.

Turnips

I make seed tapes for turnips. We use turnips in any recipe that calls for potatoes. I mash them with butter, cut them up in soup or stew, and even fry them. They are planted 4" apart in rows 12" apart. You can plant them as early as peas. They are easy to grow. I freeze them and we like them fresh. I plant Purple Top White Globe.

Plant something new and different every year. You will have some failures, but the successes are worth it. Overcoming a challenge is such a thrill. There is always a new variety in the seed catalogs. Try a different vegetable. You may love it. If you don't, compost it.

I sell enough winter squash that I pay for all my seeds. I sell enough "native" jelly and syrup that I treat myself to a new variety of fruit tree each year. The jury is still out on the Contender Peaches. They may make it or not. I think one of them sprouted from the root. Since they are grafted, that may not work out well. I have five new planting holes prepared so who knows what will catch my eye next Spring. The Saskatchewan pie cherries are a success. As long as I am able, I will garden. The whole cycle of renewal is a promise I count on.

41008967R00033